EASING
THE PAIN

*Overcoming the
Loss of a Child*

A 30-DAY DEVOTIONAL

DR. TERRA DEFOE

Published by So It Is Written, LLC
Detroit, MI
SoItIsWritten.net

Easing the Pain: Overcoming the Loss of a Child
Copyright © 2024 by Dr. Terra DeFoe

Edited by: So It Is Written – www.SoItIsWritten.net

Formatting: Ya Ya Ya Creative – YaYaYaCreative@gmail.com

ISBN: 979-8-9888204-8-2

LCCN: 2024906794

PRINTED AND BOUND IN THE UNITED STATES OF AMERICA

INTRODUCTION

Children are truly gifts from God, but what happens when the gift is taken? The crushing pain that a parent feels is indescribable. As a parent who has lost a child, I can say that I've never experienced this type of pain in my life. From the moment the doctor called to inform me of my son's time of death, I can remember it like it was yesterday. The pain was sharp and heavy. At first, I was in denial. I asked question after question, trying to make sense of what I just heard. I rehearsed over and over what I was going to say to my daughter about her brother. As much as I tried to be organized, I found myself falling apart with no one to catch me. I had become numb as I've had my fair share of trauma, loss, and grief.

Grief is tricky. Grief doesn't announce its arrival, and it certainly doesn't send a message of its departure. One day, you can find yourself in a safe space, and the next, you are left in bed feeling like you've been hit by a truck. Each day, something triggers your thoughts, reminding you that your child is no longer sharing their moments of being silly,

Dr. Terra DeFoe—EASING THE PAIN

telling jokes, attending games, and dealing with upsets and disappointments with you. Each day, you are reminded that one of your seeds is missing from the family photos. Each day you try to pick your head up, here comes a memory that knocks you back down, disrupting your thinking and your life, sending your emotions on a never-ending rollercoaster.

Easing the Pain: Overcoming the Loss of a Child 30-Day Devotional was created to help address the pain that still lives in our hearts. It doesn't matter how the child was related to you. It doesn't matter if your child didn't survive the full term of the pregnancy or died at the age of 60 years old. This devotional is designed to encourage grieving parents to find comfort in God's Word as they walk through their grief journey. This devotional will challenge you to be honest with what you are feeling and help you find permission to forgive yourself. Oftentimes, as parents, we can blame ourselves for not doing enough or not being able to help fix what caused the death of our child. Over the next 30 days, I want to share with you how God walked with me through the healing process, where I was able to replace my sorrow with joy.

DAY 1

In His hand is the life of every living creature
and the breath of all mankind.
−JOB 12:10

It could be challenging to believe that every living thing is in the hand of God. To be honest, at the moment when death visits you, words that could be mentioned can comfort your soul. The presence of friends and family should be a time that nurtures your spirit, but the dry and evil smell of death can turn your heart cold. Anyone who has lost someone special can relate to this, but losing a child magnifies this space daily. Nothing you could have done would have prepared you for this moment.

When my son passed away, I was confused about how I felt. For the first few months, I struggled to sleep and eat. It was an adjustment that didn't have an end date. I remember trying to find ways to satisfy my emotions, but nothing would work. It wasn't until I was honest with God about losing my son and the circumstances around his passing. Today, I want to remind you that God never leaves us comfortless. He is everywhere you need Him to be. Treasure the memories you have, and never let them go.

Pain to Purpose Exercise

Today, create a notebook that is between you and God. On the first page, write one word in big, bold letters that best describes the emotion you are feeling at this moment. Use up all the space on the page if needed. After you write your word, close the book and close your eyes. Allow yourself to feel whatever emotion that comes up from your stomach. Let this be the start of your healing journey with God, and watch how you will discover His love for you, which has been with you this far.

Prayer

"Father, I thank You for accepting me in whatever state I'm in. Thank You for knowing the end before I knew the beginning. Father, reveal Yourself to me and teach me how to trust You with my grief. Amen"

REFLECTION

What plan of action do you have in place to manage your grief?

_____

_____

_____

_____

_____

_____

_____

_____

_____

_____

_____

_____

_____

_____

_____

_____

_____

_____

_____

_____

_____

_____

_____

_____

_____

_____

_____

_____

_____

_____

_____

_____

_____

_____

_____

_____

_____

_____

_____

DAY 2

The Lord himself goes before you and will be with you; he will never leave you or forsake you. Do not be afraid; do not be discouraged.
—DEUTERONOMY 31:8

*H*ave you taken the time to acknowledge the pain that sits in your heart? As parents, we look to fix whatever is going wrong with our children. But when death happens or even when our child has been sentenced to prison, remember, a loss doesn't have to be permanent; the absence of our child can be felt for years. Whenever our children are out of our reach, gone from our everyday lives, there is an emptiness that makes it hard to identify our heavenly Father's presence.

God knew the very moment when your heart was troubled and broken, and He knows exactly where you are right now. When God tells us not to fear, He already knows that you would be; that was your child! Remember when you would tell your children not to do something, and they did it anyway. And when you asked them why they did it, they said, "I don't know," with those adorable, wide, soft eyes staring back at you. That's how we look to God when we become fearful. The beautiful thing about our heavenly Father is that He has gone before you to make your path to healing easier. It is never in His plan to see His children hurt, afraid, depressed, and full of anxiety, but to see you receiving His joy and peace every day you open your eyes.

Pain to Purpose Exercise

Think about a time when you believed you felt the presence of God. What was your reaction? Did you weep? Did you laugh uncontrollably? Did you stop and wonder what was that feeling? God reveals Himself to us in numerous ways. As you grow in Him, you will discover He has always been right there with you. God will never leave you alone.

Prayer

"Lord, thank You for going before us. As You guide me through this difficult journey, I will trust Your Word that You will never leave me or forsake me. Even when the pain becomes too hard for me to bear, I will not fear, for You are with me. Reveal that to me today. Amen."

REFLECTION

*Describe a time when God revealed Himself
to you during your times of trouble.*

_____

_____

_____

_____

_____

_____

_____

_____

_____

_____

_____

_____

_____

_____

_____

_____

_____

_____

_____

_____

_____

_____

_____

_____

_____

_____

_____

_____

_____

_____

_____

_____

_____

_____

DAY 3

My soul is weary with sorrow;
strengthen me according to your word!
−PSALM 119:28

*T*he day I received the call that my son was hospitalized and being prepared for ten-hour surgery, my heart felt like it fell into my stomach. He and I just spoke the night before and ended the call with, "Love you, Ma." So, I was shocked to get the call the very next day. While waiting in the emergency room all night, it wasn't until late afternoon the next day I was allowed to see my son. When I walked into the room, I was greeted with machines and a medication shelf taller than I was. Immediately, I didn't know what to ask God for. My soul took a Mike Tyson blow to the face. I didn't have the strength to stand up. My body felt like I was having hot flashes that lasted over an hour. As the doctors were explaining how and what landed my son in their care, I felt the room spinning. I thought I was about to pass out. When I walked out of the room and found a private space, I began to pray. I prayed for God to heal my son. Just that quick, I was at a loss for words. When the news went out, people around the world were praying for my son, and to this day, I thank God for them because I was on autopilot.

When you are met with a difficult circumstance, you never know how you are going to react. You will always have those who say what they would do, but when it happens, they find themselves doing the opposite. It's natural. It's perfectly fine to admit what you don't know. These are moments where God's mercy is poured over us the most. This is the moment where you can call out to God, letting go of your pride and allowing Him to strengthen you according to His Word. I learned under challenging moments like this, you can't stand on your own. God knew how to pour His strength over me because He knew I was going to need it for the long haul.

Pain to Purpose Exercise

List an emotional moment when you reacted out of anger. What did you do to calm down from that moment?

Prayer

Father, I call out to you for help. Strengthen my soul as I face this obstacle. Help me to remove my disappointment in this time of difficulty. Soften my heart and provide me with the resources and tools I need to make it through this. Open my eyes so that I can see you. Show me how to depend on you. Amen.

REFLECTION

How do you define strength? What does it look like to you?

_____

_____

_____

_____

_____

_____

_____

_____

_____

_____

_____

_____

_____

_____

_____

_____

_____

_____

_____

_____

_____

_____

_____

_____

_____

_____

_____

_____

_____

_____

_____

_____

_____

_____

_____

_____

DAY 4

Blessed are those who mourn, for they shall be comforted.
−MATTHEW 5:4

*G*rieving the loss of a child is a place of uncertainty. The depth of emotions that are felt will make you question everything around you. As a grieving parent, you will learn early that you are not the only one suffering the loss as family and friends mourn with you. It is through their love and support you will find comfort and peace. When my son passed away, there were so many moving parts that I became exhausted as people you haven't spoken to in years wanted to hear play-by-play details. People were baking cakes for me, but I didn't have the strength to eat. My family flew in just to be by my side, but I was too exhausted to sit up and talk. On one hand, my body became exhausted, but my spirit was relieved. I was relieved to be around people and not be alone. Their presence helped me take my mind off of things. Their presence helped me laugh as we discussed things that my children and their friends did, being typical teenagers. I was exhausted, but my spirit was relieved.

As you experience moments of mourning, I encourage you to take heart as God will provide you with comfort. God doesn't stop our sufferings, but He pours His glory into the littlest things. The uncertainty of how your grieving process looks is unsure, but God is not ignorant of the pain that we feel. You cannot change the sufferings, but you can change the way you think about your loss. Change the way you think about the chain of events that took place, and watch how your heart will be able to manage day after day.

Pain to Purpose Exercise

Using your notebook, write down what you would do to change the way you perceive loss.

Prayer

"Father, help me to change the way I see my suffering. Help me identify where You have placed opportunities for comfort for me to grow my trust in You. I know that Your desire is for me to be healed, but I cannot walk this journey alone. Thank You for sending me help and not leaving me to walk this path alone. Amen!"

REFLECTION

During times of grief, what does your heart want?
What do you feed it?

_____

_____

_____

_____

_____

_____

_____

_____

_____

_____

_____

_____

_____

_____

_____

_____

_____

_____

_____

_____

_____

_____

_____

_____

_____

_____

_____

_____

_____

_____

_____

_____

_____

DAY 5

Casting all your anxiety on him because he cares for you.
−1 PETER 5:7

*L*oss brings a significant flood of emotions: sadness, anger, longing, confusion, relief, loneliness, and distress, just to name a few. Parents who have lost a child are likely to experience many of these reactions and more, and they are at an increased risk for developing depression, anxiety, substance abuse, and other mental illnesses. Although grief can be exhausting, it can become overwhelming and extremely painful. Grieving is not a straight path; it's like riding a rollercoaster that's on repeat. Grieving is the stage that you have to move through and still get up the next day and go to work. You will experience moments of pain and joy. You will have moments of laughter and moments of extreme madness.

There isn't a timeline for your grief. Ten years later, I find myself facing moments of anxiety. I still experience moments where my body hurts, and it's difficult for me to get out of bed, but I've developed a plan that keeps me from going down the rabbit hole. When God says to cast all our cares and anxieties on Him, He means just that. The enemy loves to live in the dark. When you are holding on to the pain and anxiety, you allow the enemy to keep you in a box. God will help you in your weakness.

Pain to Purpose Exercise

What anxiety are you feeling today? In two sentences, how would you describe your anxiety level today?

Prayer

"Lord, I do not know what to pray for, but I'm giving You my cares. My cares are _____ _____. As I call out my cares or as I write out my cares, I pray that You will intercede on my behalf. Lord, thank You for taking care of me and lifting this burden off my shoulders. Caring around my cares is weighing me down, and that is not Your will for my life. Amen."*

REFLECTION

Is there something you are focusing on that is creating your anxiety? I suggest you focus on the solution.

_____

_____

_____

_____

_____

_____

_____

_____

_____

_____

_____

_____

_____

_____

_____

DAY 6

Come to me, all you who are weary and burdened,
and I will give you rest.
−MATTHEW 11:28

"*It* has been years, and I should be in a better place by now." Stop trying to time your grief. Grief within itself can cause a variety of mental and physiological responses. Sometimes, you can add more stress trying to find an end date for your grief. As a project manager, I tried to approach my grief like a project that I could manage. I am the type of person who likes deadlines. When I deal with it, it's considered dealt with and over. I have developed these enteral processes to protect my mental health, and for the most part, it has worked. The problem is that grief doesn't work like that. The emotions and reactions that come along with grieving don't have deadlines. Now, knowing this, I had to incorporate a system where the yoke of grief would not take over me. I encourage you to release the grief that is causing you pain.

God knows that the loss is going to cause you pain. He is not surprised by the stages that you will face. This is why

He tells us to cast our burden on Him. Your burdens are not limited to the lack of money or things that we can touch. God knows the burden of unforgiveness, the burden of guilt, the burden of being misunderstood, and the burden of not trusting Him. God encourages you to give Him your cares, and in return, He will give you His yoke that is easy and light. God didn't say it would be over; He said it would be light. God taught me to give Him my anxiety, give Him my anger, give Him my frustration, and in return, He will give me His love, His peace, and the ability to manage through the madness. If I had given up on my life during my times of suffering, I never would be able to share with you that God is right with you. His power can reach down into the pit and guide you into all truth.

Pain to Purpose Exercise

Write down three words that best describe the burdens caused by your loss.

Prayer

"Father, there is no pain that I am experiencing that is a surprise to you. Lord, I want to give You my burdens. I want to give You my pain. Lord, teach me, guide me right now, show me how to give You my burden, and in return, I will take Your yoke that is made easy for me. I thank You in advance for cutting off the spirit of bondage that is trying to take over my life. Amen."

REFLECTION

Do you find it hard to release your pain?
If your grief had a name, what would it be?

_____

_____

_____

_____

_____

_____

_____

_____

_____

_____

_____

_____

_____

_____

_____

DAY 7

The Lord is close to the brokenhearted and
saves those who are crushed in spirit.
−PSALM 34:18

The loss of a child can be a crushing experience that can make you suffer in silence. After a month, everyone returned to their normal lives. They say a prayer for you. They may call and text, but they have moved on. Yes, you get up and go to work every day. Yes, you preach every Sunday. Yes, you are still running your business, but the suffering eats silently at your soul. You are not alone. Hanna grieved because her womb remained closed for years (1 Samuel 1:1-16). Hagar sobbed in the desert as her son was about to die (Genesis 21:15-16). Jonah was angry with God to the point of death (Jonah 4:3-9). God has a way of fixing our broken hearts. Because He is God, He uses anything and everyone. As I was learning to walk through my forest, I had to get to the place where I had to strip down from being a superwoman and acknowledge that my spirit had a hole in it. When you have that intimate moment with God, He reveals a side of Him that you heard from others. He gives you access to a world of peace that changes your appearance.

Today, I encourage you to end this week by casting your cares on God. As we end this week, give God what's in your heart: the good, the bad, and the ugly. You don't have to play Superman or Superwoman another day. If you took on substance to ease your pain, give it to God. If you took on sexual pleasures to fill the void, give it to God. If you are honest, those things didn't even help your pain.

Pain to Purpose Exercise

In three sentences, describe what you learned from this week as it relates to casting your cares on God. Write down three words that best describe the burdens caused by your loss.

Prayer

"Lord, I may not understand what I'm about to say, but Lord, I need to take off the mask that I have been wearing to show others that I am managing my grief, but today it stops. I lay aside my garments of grief, anger, depression, unforgiveness, bitterness, and any other thing that is sitting in my heart. Thank you, Lord, that I can trust you with my exposed face. Amen."

REFLECTION

Can you identify the moment when your heart became broken?
How did you manage to cope?

_____

_____

_____

_____

_____

_____

_____

_____

_____

_____

_____

_____

_____

_____

_____

DAY 8

Be merciful on me, Lord, for I am distress; my eyes grow weak
with sorrow, my soul and body with grief.
−PSALM 31:9

*D*id you know that when you experience grief, it can worsen existing chronic mental health and immune system dysfunctions? Incorporating self-care into your daily routine is important for your overall health. Regular exercise can help reduce stress, feelings of anxiety, and symptoms of depression while boosting your self-esteem and happiness. Eating healthy will build your body's defenses, which it needs to fight feelings of sadness. Highly processed or deep-fried foods tend to leave you feeling down. This is why medical professionals warn against unhealthy eating, as it plays an essential role in your mental health.

Over the past four years, my nonprofit organization has partnered with local recreation centers to host one-hour trauma, loss, and grief yoga therapy sessions. These sessions are open to the public and offered for free. We found that post-COVID-19, many people experienced loss on every level, and we wanted to ensure that they had a safe environment to release their grief. We believe that small volumes of physical movement are critical to the mind, body, and spirit. God wants you to be whole and healthy. In His creations, we can find opportunities for relief if we seek them. Today, know that God's mercy will lift you out of any state that you may be experiencing. Trust Him to help you.

Pain to Purpose Exercise

Take a moment and close your eyes. Think of a place or memory that makes you happy. Take a slow, deep breath through your nose. Now, slowly exhale the breath through your mouth. If you like, blow as hard as you can. Try this technique every time you feel anxious.

Prayer

"Father, I thank You for a quiet moment with You. Teach me how to take care of myself the way You will have me to. Show me where I can improve on being kind to myself. Amen."

REFLECTION

When was the last time you did something for yourself?
Learn to schedule something for yourself
daily that is between you and God.

_____

_____

_____

_____

_____

_____

_____

_____

_____

_____

_____

_____

_____

_____

_____

DAY 9

He lifted me out of the slimy pit, out of the mud and mire;
he set my feet on a rock and gave me a firm place to stand.
−PSALM 40:2

*F*riend, I know that it is not easy having to be in this space. You prayed, and yet your request was unanswered. You are faced with a circumstance that is more than you can mentally manage. The more you press through the sleepless nights and frustrating mornings, the more you feel overwhelmed, and you feel yourself hitting rock bottom.

Losing a child can be one of the most challenging things you can ever experience, or having to receive the initial phone call to identify your child's body. We had to select their last suit or dress and see their photo on the cover of an obituary, had to say goodbye for the last time, and had to put their death certificate next to their birth certificate. No one and nothing prepared you for the agony that you are feeling. During this time, I strongly encourage you to seek help before your behavior finds comfort in unhealthy alternatives such as excessive sex, disruptive use of alcohol, prescription pills, and street drugs. As humans, we naturally search for ways to release, stuff down, and mask our pain. We tell ourselves that we are "good" when we are suffering inside. We keep it to ourselves because we have to show others that we are strong. Today, allow yourself the opportunity to be weak and allow God to be strong (2 Corinthians 12:9). Stop trying to manage God's job. You cannot face this in your capabilities.

Pain to Purpose Exercise

Identify three things that you have used to mask your grief. Write them down in a sentence.

Prayer

"Lord, I know that using material things to relieve my pain is not good for me and for those I love. Father, I need Your help; I cannot stop this behavior on my own. There are so many memories, and I need Your strength to move forward. Forgive me for my bad behavior, and thank You for getting me through my negative habits. I know that I am in a safe space in You. In Jesus' name, amen."

REFLECTION

Do you find yourself wanting to mask your behavior to avoid facing your challenges? What are ways you can adopt outside activities that can help preoccupy your time?

_____

_____

_____

_____

_____

_____

_____

_____

_____

_____

_____

_____

_____

_____

DAY 10

A person's steps are directed by the Lord.
How then can anyone understand their own way?
−PROVERBS 20:24

What doubt do you have that God cannot help you? Since you have been in control of your emotions and behavior, where has that gotten you? The words you use during this season of your life can have profound outcomes on everything you do moving forward. In fact, it has a direct connection to the pain you are feeling right now. The words from others that you have collected in your mind can leave you in worse shape than you can imagine.

When my son passed away, I had to be careful about my actions. I knew that if I reacted to the things people said and were doing, I knew that it wasn't going to end well for me. I had a lot riding on every decision. People will push you into a corner, and the enemy will use anything against you to make you miss a step. Because God knows the paths we take, He is not surprised by what we do. I encourage you to make sure you allow God to direct your steps. When people are not on their best behavior, take a moment to breathe and reevaluate the situation later. Do not allow them to win.

Pain to Purpose Exercise

Take a few minutes to breathe. Find a quiet space where you can take five deep breaths. Allow this moment to serve as time to clear your mind and heart.

Prayer

"Father, I do not want the things that people say to infect my spirit. Help me to reject every negative word and action that has been done against me. Teach me how to receive Your words of life to water my soul. Refresh my thoughts so that I can be revived in You. Amen."

REFLECTION

How do you react when people say negative things to you?
How long do you hold onto grudges?

_____

_____

_____

_____

_____

_____

_____

_____

_____

_____

_____

_____

_____

_____

DAY 11

"For my thoughts are not your thoughts,
neither are your ways my ways," declares the Lord.
−ISAIAH 55:8

*O*ften, we try to take matters into our own hands. We try to deal with loss and grief on our own. We believe we can suck it up and just move on. Unresolved feelings of sadness only prolong what you will not face. Remember, you are not the only person to face this challenge. Do you know how many people have been where you are right now? Everyone who has stood on this stage can tell you that it is not the prettiest place to be, but you can get through it when you face it. There is nothing stylish, glamorous, or fun about grieving. It is a lonely, dark, and unpredictable space. Every day brings new emotions. There is not one single day that is the same.

As I was slipping into a foggy place, I learned quickly that I had to face this challenge regardless of how I felt. I had to stop kicking the can down the street, thinking it would just blow over. I found myself praying and praying, but God was not answering my prayers the way I thought He would. God was teaching me about forgiveness, humility, patience, and gratitude. I was not expecting these lessons during a time when I was asking God to remove my pain, strengthen my heart, and give me peace. God's ways were not my ways, and His thoughts were not my thoughts. The more He was teaching me, the more I looked at my circumstances differently. I was able to use the things He taught me in every challenge that I faced, which built my strength and faith walk.

Pain to Purpose Exercise

Think about a time when God handled your situation in a way that was different from what you thought He would. Write down what you learned from that experience.

Prayer

"Father, I may not understand Your thoughts and ways, but position me to accept Your instructions as You know what is best for me. In Jesus' name, amen."

REFLECTION

Are you holding back from following an instruction that you were given because of fear? What did you learn from it?

_____

_____

_____

_____

_____

_____

_____

_____

_____

_____

_____

_____

_____

_____

_____

DAY 12

He rescues me unharmed from the battle waged against me,
even though many oppose me.
−PSALM 55:18

The five phases of grief can manifest differently in every person. Denial, anger, bargaining, depression, and integration/acceptance are all developed after a loss or death. When grieving is eliminated from conversations or portrayed as a complex mental disorder, we miss the opportunity for those who are suffering to locate the proper resources, and with this, many people are misdiagnosed. Their moment for healing and recovery decreases.

Culturally, we tend to underestimate the trauma that a parent is experiencing. When you are fighting anxiety for a long period, it can become exhausting, and this is when other mental health challenges can surface. Through your moments of grieving, make it a habit to take steps to combat those unwanted emotions. During COVID-19, I started a six-week Trauma, Loss, and Grief Recovery Program. Sessions were for one hour via Zoom on Saturday mornings and Thursday evenings. During these sessions, we would discuss various topics, complete exercises, and watch topic-related videos. These sessions were designed to assist those who were struggling and felt isolated due to the pandemic to overcome their anxiety and reprogram their path toward healing. I strongly encourage you to join a support group or participate in a healthy activity such as devotionals like this. The ability to journal your thoughts and challenge your thinking will help your heart and mind and refresh your spirit.

Pain to Purpose Exercise

Search for peer support groups in your area. Read their websites and identify how many groups are grieving-focused. Pick one and consider attending.

Prayer

"Lord, as I look for resources to assist me on this journey, lead me to the suitable method of support You would have for me. Connect me with the right group of people. Amen."

REFLECTION

Are you allowing fear to hijack your healing journey? If so, why?

_____

_____

_____

_____

_____

_____

_____

_____

_____

_____

_____

_____

_____

_____

_____

DAY 13

I consider that our present sufferings are not worth comparing with the glory that will be revealed in us.
−ROMANS 8:18

Sometimes, when I think back to that day compared to where I am now, I must say, "I can see clearly now that the rain is gone." Don't get me wrong, I have moments when I cry thinking about my son, or I find myself laughing at something he said or did. There are times I dream about my son and wake up crying. The quiet times when I'm left to my thoughts, I find that the time through the years has gotten easier.

If you ask me, "Did the suffering make you stronger?" Yes! I believe my suffering strengthens my relationship and dependency on God. It increased my personal growth and awareness. I believe that those who suffer significant loss develop resilience. To grow healthy, beautiful green grass, you must test your soil, use the right fertilizer, kill the weeds, and use fresh grass seeds, then water to bring nourishment. When the time comes, do not be afraid. Remember, you are growing healthy green grass.

Pain to Purpose Exercise

Write down three ways you can use your loss for good.

Prayer

"Father, teach me how to develop resilience from my suffering. Show me how to find the good in my suffering and what You want me to do with it. Thank You for bringing me to this place and not leaving me alone. In Jesus' name, amen."

REFLECTION

From that moment to now, what areas have you seen growth in your personal and spiritual life?

_____

_____

_____

_____

_____

_____

_____

_____

_____

_____

_____

_____

_____

_____

_____

_____

_____

_____

_____

DAY 14

So with you: Now is your time of grief, but I will see you again
and you will rejoice, and no one will take away your joy.
—JOHN 16:22

For some people, grief and joy shouldn't be in the same sentence, but why not? I grieved every Mother's Day, my son's birthday, and the day they officially called his death. Some years were harder than others, but as time passed, my grief turned into rejoicing. As I found joy, I understood that it didn't negate the need to express sadness.

You will never land on the yellow brick road trying to escape or bypass grief. A loss is real life, and in real life, you are experiencing pain. In real life, fighting yourself to push past this moment is unwise and unhealthy. God will provide you with everything you need to survive this journey. He will send people, reading materials like this, sermons, songs, poems, pets, hobbies, and anything else He needs to remind you that this pain is for a moment; joy is coming.

Pain to Purpose Exercise

Describe a moment since reading this devotional when you have experienced joy. Write down how it made you feel.

Prayer

"Lord, I want to experience the joy You have designed for me. Help me to become aware when You are releasing your joy in my life. Amen."

REFLECTION

What does joy look like in your life?

_____

_____

_____

_____

_____

_____

_____

_____

_____

_____

_____

_____

_____

_____

_____

_____

DAY 15

He will wipe away every tear from their eyes.
There will be no more death or mourning or crying or pain,
for the old order of things has passed away.
−REVELATION 21:4

*F*inding the strength to pray when grief is present can be a challenge. It can be difficult to find the words to say to God when your heart is heavy and lacks motivation. In times like this, we need God more than ever. On our own, we do not understand every detail of our lives. We try to analyze the fragmented pieces of our broken hearts while trying to make sense of the pain and disappointment.

I remember times when I couldn't cry about the loss of my son, even when I wanted to. Yes, I couldn't cry; not a tear would form. It was hard for me to understand at first, but I learned that the more I was honest with God about my disappointment, the more He was honest with me about His healing power. Moments when I was confused, God gave me clarity. Moments when I was discouraged, He gave me strength. Moments when my pain was unbearable, God wrapped me in His love. I was grateful that His mercy touched me far beyond my thoughts. Today, when the tears are flowing down your face with a shattered heart, move closer to God. This is a perfect moment to play your worship music, recite your favorite bible scriptures, or simply talk to Him. He is waiting to hear from you.

Pain to Purpose Exercise

Take ten minutes to listen to your favorite worship songs or try listening to a few new ones. Write down three things that you are grateful for that God has done for you since your loss.

Prayer

"Father, You said in Your Word that You will wipe away every tear from my eyes. As the tears flow, help me see the good in my pain. Help me to feel comfort in my discomfort. Help me to see Your love through my loneliness. As I face this day, be with me. Amen."

REFLECTION

What are the thoughts that trigger your tears?
How do you draw closer to God?

_____

_____

_____

_____

_____

_____

_____

_____

_____

_____

_____

_____

_____

_____

_____

_____

DAY 16

Cast your cares on the Lord and He will sustain you;
He will never let the righteous be shaken.
−PSALM 55:22

hrough God's Word, we are grounded in faith and hope. God shares His love and support during our difficult times as a sign that He is with us. God is sympathetic to our pain. He understands and is right there with you. He knows that we will never get over our loss; we will never get over the pain, but He does offer a path for us to not get stuck there.

It was years before I arrived at a place where my tears of pain turned into tears of joy. When I talk about my son to others, I no longer hold my head down and go into a soft, weak voice. I laugh when I talk about him. I share stories about my son with others freely. God allowed me to use my grief to help others overcome theirs. I understand how you can give up hope. I understand how you can suffer in silence. When I noticed that my grief had attacked my body, I knew I was in trouble, and I needed to turn the corner fast.

When you hand your cares to God, He will take them and exchange them with His strength that will sustain you.

Pain to Purpose Exercise

Write down the names of three people you think would benefit from this devotional. Text them a scripture from the devotional once a week for the next four weeks and track their response.

Prayer

"Lord, as I continue to give You my cares, give me a double portion of Your strength to sustain me so that I don't fall. Let not my grief become bait for the enemy to use against me. Teach me how to stand firmly on Your Word. Amen."

REFLECTION

How does it make you feel when you are open with God about your emotions? Do you feel His support and strength?

_____

_____

_____

_____

_____

_____

_____

_____

_____

_____

_____

_____

_____

_____

_____

_____

DAY 17

Heal me, Lord, and I will be healed; save me and
I will be saved, for you are the one I praise.
−JEREMIAH 17:14

*D*avid pleaded with God for the life of his son.
David fasted, went into his house, and spent nights
lying on the ground, calling out to God to plead for his life.
There were times when David refused to get off the ground
as the elders tried to get him up. David went days without
eating and drinking, pleading God for the life of his son. On
the seventh day, David's son died. (2 Samuel 12:17-20)

I think we all can relate to David's position. Our hearts
cried to God, pleading for the health and well-being of our
children. As we did not receive the outcome we desired, we
reached that place as David. The Bible says, "Then David
got up from the ground. After he had washed, put on
lotions, and changed his clothes, he went into the house of
the Lord and worshipped. Then he went to his own house,
and at his request, they served him food, and he ate." God
has a way of starting the process of healing our broken
hearts. Your process may not be the same as mine and

others, but the process has started. God cares about every detail of your life. Today, take hold of His strength that will cover and save you.

Pain to Purpose Exercise

Write down the names of the areas that you want God to heal and ask Him to heal you.

Prayer

"Father, help me to get off the ground. Help me walk in victory as I take this journey. I believe You can heal me. Help me from falling prey to my self-destructive thoughts that are not producing good results in my life. I receive Your healing in Jesus' name, amen."

REFLECTION

Are you surrounded by people to encourage your healing in a godly fashion? Do you feel supported by those around you?

_____

_____

_____

_____

_____

_____

_____

_____

_____

_____

_____

_____

_____

_____

DAY 18

Then Jesus told him, "Because you have seen me, you have believed;
blessed are those who have not seen and yet have believed."
—JOHN 20:29

It is not unusual to feel isolated and helpless. Grieving the loss of a child can take your mind to places you never thought it could go. Even though you are praying, you may not always receive the answers you desire at the time. Sometimes, there is a delay in God's response because we are not ready to receive them. During moments like these, do not give up praying. Do not give up seeking God. Do not give up giving God your burdens. In a short time, you will receive what God has to say to you.

Sometimes, we are dependent on the things we see, but we ignore the things that cannot be seen. Thomas was waiting on the evidence that Jesus had returned. Thomas did something that we are all guilty of; he doubted Jesus, but he also asked Him to help his unbelief. When God reveals His promise to comfort and heal you, do not doubt Him. Everything will become clear soon. Just keep believing.

Pain to Purpose Exercise

Write down what you are asking God to answer. How are you positioning yourself for the answer?

Prayer

"Father, help me to hear what You have to say to me. Forgive me for any unforgiveness that I may be holding in my heart. Amen."

REFLECTION

Do you have a specific way God speaks to you? How would you prefer God to speak to you? Explain why.

_____

_____

_____

_____

_____

_____

_____

_____

_____

_____

_____

_____

_____

_____

_____

DAY 19

Then Jesus said, "Did I not tell you that if you believe,
you will see the glory of God?"
—JOHN 11:40

There were moments when I felt that God stopped hearing my prayers and was ignoring me. God's silence during times when grief was present was not the best, but I learned something... God was building me to make it through those difficult times. He was showing me His glory even when I didn't feel Him nearby. During those times, I made time to pray, cut off distractions, and recited those scriptures that encouraged my heart. God was teaching me to trust Him and to stand on His Word.

My relationship became intimate over time, and it was the best thing that ever happened to me. As I managed through my day-to-day living, there were moments when the emotional pain was complex. It was in those times I had to go back and shift my focus to surviving the storms. I believed that I could, and I did, and God revealed His glory.

Pain to Purpose Exercise

Write down a moment you instructed your child, and they followed it. How did it make you feel?

Prayer

"Lord, today I ask You to allow me to see Your glory. Teach me how to depend on You as I experience these moments of grief. Amen."

REFLECTION

Have you ever felt that God has forgotten about you? Does the feeling of absence develop during your times of grieving?

_____

_____

_____

_____

_____

_____

_____

_____

_____

_____

_____

_____

_____

_____

_____

_____

DAY 20

I will repay to you the years the locusts have eaten-the great
locust and the young locust, the other locusts and the
swarm-my great army that I sent among you.
—JOEL 2:25

*T*hrough His promise of grace, God will restore all that was eaten from you in the loss of your child. The dreadful nights and the painful mornings. All the time that you cried alone, asking Him, "Why?" God can restore! God can restore years of suffering in silence. God can restore you mentally, physically, and financially.

There were times when I used retail shopping as a source of therapy. I tried to shop my way out of grief. By doing this, it affected my budget and threw me into a deeper depression. It took a year for me to get back on track financially to meet my financial obligations without being sued. I wouldn't recommend this path to anyone. Shopping may allow you moments of relief, but it's going to come back to bite you later. I had to swallow my pride and ask God for forgiveness. He gave me direction on managing my finances, but most importantly, He taught me how to lean on Him in my times of grief. In return, God strengthened my soul, and day by day, He has restored the years that grief had eaten.

Pain to Purpose Exercise

Write three things grief has eaten in your life, then ask God to restore them.

Prayer

"Lord, thank You for helping me to identify areas of my life where grief has eaten away. Lord, restore and repair the years that were eaten. Help me to reclaim my time and teach me how to overcome grief so that it doesn't continue to eat away my soul. In Jesus' name, amen."

REFLECTION

*What can you do today to restore your
time of self-destructive behavior?*

_____

_____

_____

_____

_____

_____

_____

_____

_____

_____

_____

_____

_____

DAY 21

But those who hope in the Lord will renew their strength.
They will soar on wings like eagles; they will run and
not grow weary, they will walk and not be faint.
—ISAIAH 40:31

*H*ave you ever sat and watched an eagle fly? The flying power of an eagle is 20-40 miles per hour in normal flight and can dive at speeds of 75-100 mph. Their flight altitudes are 10,000 feet or more, and they can soar in the air for hours riding on natural wind currents. That's pretty amazing! It is the eagle's wings that allow it to navigate through the air and ride the wind, moving at a speed similar to an airplane. Can you imagine having renewed strength strong enough to lift you 10,000 feet in the sky?

When you wait on God, He will boost your level of trust, confidence, and reassurance. God will give you the strength to overcome every negative circumstance that grief brings. The more you give Him your anxiety, the more He will give you courage, building your faith more and more. As you build your self-confidence through His Word, watch God renew your energy, renew your sense of purpose, and renew your hope.

Pain to Purpose Exercise

Name two things you need to overcome today. Write them down and repeat them to yourself. What was your experience?

Prayer

"Father, I trust that You will renew Your strength and restore my sense of purpose. Teach me how to recognize when I'm flying like an eagle. Thank You for teaching me how to fly higher than my challenges. Amen."

REFLECTION

Do you feel your wings mounting?
What can you do today to prepare to fly?

_____

_____

_____

_____

_____

_____

_____

_____

_____

_____

_____

_____

_____

_____

_____

_____

DAY 22

For his anger lasts only a moment, but his favor lasts a lifetime;
weeping may stay for the night, but rejoicing comes in the morning.
—PSALM 30:5

Don't be confused if you find yourself weeping during times of sadness but feeling joyful. Expressing grief and experiencing happiness is the best way I can describe moments I had. There were times when my pain was physically hurting my body, but I had the strength to lift my hands to the Lord, praising Him for His mercy. My soul was vexed, but my spirit rejoiced.

God has a way of sending your senses into complexity. This can serve as an indicator that He has you covered. You may go to bed feeling sad and alone while crying yourself to sleep, but in the morning, you will rejoice. Through the night, when your body is resting, I believe He reminds our spirit of His promises. With His still, soft voice, He commands authority over our hearts and minds, flushing out disruptive thoughts and emotions. Instead of leaving us to fight for ourselves, God refines us, renews us, and reconciles us.

Pain to Purpose Exercise

When was the last time you cried through a joyful moment? Describe how you felt.

Prayer

"Father, thank You for the joy that comes in the morning. Reveal to me how to recognize when Your joy has replaced my sorrow. In Jesus' name, amen."

REFLECTION

What can you offer yourself to experience joy?

_____

_____

_____

_____

_____

_____

_____

_____

_____

_____

_____

_____

_____

_____

_____

_____

DAY 23

For the Spirit God gave us does not make us timid,
but gives us power, love and self-discipline.
−2 TIMOTHY 1:7

*G*od can restore you in every area of your life after the loss of a child. Trusting God while you are suffering in silence can be difficult. You want to believe His Word. You want to praise Him with your whole heart, but deep down inside, there is a part of you that is lost. There is a part of you that died with your child. Nothing that you have done on purpose, but your spirit has been disappointed. You didn't wake up today not wanting to trust Him, but the pain is so strong that you can't bring yourself to rejoice.

There were times when I enjoyed going to church. I looked forward to attending bible study, but there was a part of my heart that had an invisible scar that I didn't want people to see. My smiles became less, and my laughter faded away; that's when I would feel God wrapping His arms around me. Through the hugs and kind words of others,

God restored my heart and helped me regain my passion for Him.

Pain to Purpose Exercise

Write down three things you need God to restore and why?

Prayer

"Father, my heart isn't where it should be. Lift this grieving scar from me so that I can be restored. Amen."

REFLECTION

How important is your relationship with God?
Do you believe that He can restore your joy?

_____

_____

_____

_____

_____

_____

_____

_____

_____

_____

_____

_____

_____

_____

_____

_____

_____

DAY 24

Though He brings grief, He will show compassion,
so great is His unfailing love.
–LAMENTATIONS 3:32

*T*he ability to cope with grief is an experience far too many parents have to face. It is extremely difficult to grieve while having to function in everyday life. I don't know if my level of compassion would be this sensitive if I had not experienced the loss of my child. Trying to maintain focus and rebuild my space, knowing that my son will never celebrate future life-changing moments and accomplishments with me.

As grief is a normal and acceptable response to the loss of a loved one, rebuilding healthy emotional and behavioral boundaries by participating in social activities can reduce the side effects of grief. I remember the first Mother's Day after losing my son; I bought Mother's Day balloons for all the mothers on my floor at work. Even though I was torn apart, I wanted to share the excitement and joy that Mother's Day brings, so I decided to celebrate them. You will be surprised what small acts of kindness will do for a crying soul. Seeing the smiles on their faces renewed my strength.

Pain to Purpose Exercise

Write down a small act of kindness and do it anonymously for a parent who shares the same emotional pain as you.

Prayer

"Lord, help me to have compassion for others who may be where I am. Help me to encourage them along their journey as You have taught me through Your Word. In Jesus' name, amen."

REFLECTION

What are you doing right now to show compassion to others?

_____

_____

_____

_____

_____

_____

_____

_____

_____

_____

_____

_____

_____

_____

_____

_____

_____

_____

_____

_____

_____

_____

_____

_____

_____

_____

_____

_____

_____

_____

_____

_____

_____

_____

_____

_____

Day 25

I can do all things through him who gives me strength.
−PHILIPPIANS 4:13

The crossroad between trusting God while grieving the loss of a child can be confusing. On the one hand, you are trying to stand strong in your faith, and on the other hand, you are in emotional and physical pain. I wrestled with this daily. On the days I forced myself out of bed, my thoughts were not positive. I had to return to work and focus on projects that I was assigned to. My mental state was challenged. I struggled with reading basic information and having to write emails. I felt like I was in a fog trying to function at a level I lost before my son passed, but I had to get up! I had to push my way through. A few months later, I suffered a panic attack, which we learned later. If that was a panic attack, I do not want to know what a heart attack felt like. My daughter had to rush me to the hospital, and they ran test after test. I remember the doctor asking me if I had experienced any trauma over the past few months. Extreme trauma can trigger panic and anxiety attacks that will affect your health. Things that are eating at your peace, your rest, and your emotions, your body will react to the pressure sooner or later.

To convince my doctor not to put me on blood pressure medication, I had to get things off my chest and fast. One morning, I found myself at my local high school track, where I ran in the rain for hours, crying. Releasing the bondage of hurt, disappointment, and shame will allow you to release the heaviness that you carry. When you have resentment, it can be an open door for the enemy to play with your thoughts. I had to let go of grudges against others and forgive them. After I cut those chains, my mental and emotional health was restored. I learned that I could let it go and give it to God.

Pain to Purpose Exercise

Write down a word that best describes the bondage that is harboring in your heart.

Prayer

"Lord, I want to release the bondage that is holding me back. Show me who I need to forgive and set me free from them. Amen."

REFLECTION

During your moments of anxiety, what do you feel?
How do you find relief?

_____

_____

_____

_____

_____

_____

_____

_____

_____

_____

_____

_____

_____

_____

_____

DAY 26

My flesh and my heart may fail,
but God is the strength of my heart and my portion forever.
−PSALM 73:26

*H*ave you experienced a time when your mind became overwhelmed, and fear was present in every situation you were in? The anxiety that you experience is a hint that you need strength and peace from God. As a Believer, the challenges we face in life come to attack our flesh and cause separation from the love and protection of God. Friend, please understand that God is bigger than your anxiety. God is bigger than the ways you find yourself self-medicating. God's love for you is more than anything I can describe; it's an experience that He wants to have one-on-one with you.

It is natural for your flesh to fight against God's instructions to manage your fears and troubles. To fix or put things to rest, you have to be willing to face it. When you face it, your troubles can no longer be hidden. You will find the strength to face the moments when your heart fails.

God will give you the right amount of strength to walk through every situation.

Pain to Purpose Exercise

List three areas where you need God to strengthen your walk with Him.

Prayer

"Father, I need your strength as I walk a path that I don't understand. Lord, I renounce my anxiety and receive Your love. Thank You for not leaving me to fix my life on my own. Amen."

REFLECTION

What decision can you make today to
strengthen your walk with God?

_____

_____

_____

_____

_____

_____

_____

_____

_____

_____

_____

_____

_____

_____

_____

DAY 27

Have I not commanded you? Be strong and courageous.
Do not be afraid; do not be discouraged,
for the Lord your God will be with you wherever you go!
—JOSHUA 1:9

God has commanded you to be strong and courageous. He has commanded you to possess, face, and deal with danger or fear without flinching. There is a reason God commanded us to be strong and courageous because He knows that you can. When grief presented itself, I wanted to be prepared to face it without fear. I didn't want to keep experiencing the pain or anticipating the pain to arrive. When Mother's Day came, I took a trip out of town to a place where I found peace. I traveled alone so that I could get what I needed from God. I booked a massage and plan a time to go sightseeing. I refused to lay in bed rehearsing thoughts that would escort me into fear and depression. When my son's birthday came, my daughter and I went out for a bike ride and dinner, then ended the day by watching one of my son's favorite movies. We decided to reflect on the good times. I learned how to equip myself with the tools I needed to push back feelings of sadness. When the holidays came, I could feel the anxiety rising. Still, I found opportunities to show love and kindness to others.

When you are busy with ways to bless others, it decreases your levels of anxiety. Please note that it took me years to develop this routine. This is nothing that happened overnight. I had to learn how to put one foot in front of the other. I learned who I can call to pray with me. I had to learn what scriptures to repeat to strengthen my spirit. Now, I travel to my Mother's Day spot with family and friends. God will give you a village of people to support you on your healing journey. Today, know that God is with you as you continue your healing journey. God knows what is inside you, and you will become fruitful in everything you do.

Pain to Purpose Exercise

List how you celebrate the life of your child. How has that grown?

Prayer

"Father, equip me to be strong and courageous. Show me in Your Word where others were faced with troubles, and You gave them strength. Amen."

REFLECTION

*Who can you turn to that gives you strength during
your time of grief? What tools do you use to help
you get out of the rabbit hole?*

_____

_____

_____

_____

_____

_____

_____

_____

_____

_____

_____

_____

_____

_____

_____

DAY 28

When you pass through the waters, I will be with you;
and when you pass through the rivers, they will not sweep over
you. When you walk through the fire, you will not be burned;
the flames will not set you ablaze.
—ISAIAH 43:2

*T*his scripture is the glue that keeps me together. This scripture has been a lifevest for me through every traumatic experience I've faced, and I pray that it will become one of yours. In life, we will face moments that we did not see coming. In this scripture, God provides a hidden closet where you can take shelter in Him. When you are feeling troubled and unsure, remember that God will not allow the circumstance to sweep over you, and no matter how hot it gets, the flames will not burn you.

This brings me to Shadrach, Meshach, and Abednego. In the book of Daniel, the three Jewish men were thrown into a fiery furnace by Nebuchadnezzar II, the King of Babylon, for refusing to bow to the king's image. These young men believed that God would deliver them out of the king's hands, and He did. When you are committed to standing on God's promises through your actions, it will reveal the value of your beliefs. I encourage you to stand on God's promises and commit to putting grief in its rightful place. As you understand the risk involved with fear, anxiety, and sadness, make the necessary life changes to hand your cares to God and, in exchange, receive His love, peace, and joy.

Pain to Purpose Exercise

Write the steps you are willing to take to walk your path toward healing.

Prayer

"*Father, I thank You for not allowing the rivers to overtake me. Thank You for not allowing the flames to burn me. Continue to walk with me as I pull the pieces of my life back together. In Jesus' name, amen.*"

REFLECTION

Moving forward, how will you acknowledge the presence of God?
How will you maintain building a relationship with Him?

_____

_____

_____

_____

_____

_____

_____

_____

_____

_____

_____

_____

_____

_____

_____

_____

DAY 29

So do not fear, for I am with you; do not be dismayed,
for I am your God. I will strengthen you and help you;
I will uphold you with my righteous right hand.
—ISAIAH 41:10

The moment I decided to walk by faith when faced with grief and anxiety flashbacks, I learned that I was fighting fear. I was fighting against something that wasn't taught to me. Often, when we become fearful and anxious, we are fighting something we are afraid to face. I encourage you to stop worrying about the next time conflict enters your heart. Use the tools from this devotional to develop a strategy to arm yourself to face the challenge.

When I would become fearful, I used to worry myself into a migraine headache. I did things like picking with my right ear or aggressively biting the inside of my lip. I would do those things until the point of drawing blood. After the second year of the passing of my son, I decided I was going to get rid of my pain by lying on a tattoo table. Six hours later, I was marked with art that covered half of my body. The pain from the needles flushed the emotional pain I was feeling at that time, which became unbearable. I later learned that it didn't benefit me at all. Those are just a few examples of how anxiety can manifest into the physical. Through various teachings, I learned to shift my thoughts through prayer and meditation by visualizing positive outcomes, incorporating exercise, painting, yoga, and socializing with family and friends more often. Unfortunately, grieving can have the same effects on you physically and mentally, just like sicknesses and diseases. When you overcome rational thoughts, you will begin to see a difference when grief approaches. Stay encouraged! You are not alone!

Pain to Purpose Exercise

List three people who encourage you during your moments of grief and why.

Prayer

"Lord, sometimes the pain seems to get harder day after day. Help me to see the good in my current sufferings. Help me to stop expecting the worst and experience the good You have for me. The moment grief surfaces in my heart, show me what to do. Thank You for keeping me in Your right hand."

REFLECTION

What are some past methods you have used to cope with grief?
Did those methods work?

_____

_____

_____

_____

_____

_____

_____

_____

_____

_____

_____

_____

_____

_____

_____

_____

DAY 30

Little by little, I will drive them out before you, until you have
increased enough to take possession of the land.
−EXODUS 23:30

As you continue on your healing journey, remember this is not a sprint but a marathon. Little by little, you will notice the days are getting easier. Little by little, you will gain strength through God's Word, maintaining a self-care routine, and welcoming your emotions to grief the loss of your child. This is not a fire drill but a real-life natural experience you are having. I encourage you to be kind to yourself and check the negative thoughts at the door.

You will find the more you identify the grief triggers, the more you can apply your devotional teachings to navigate you through those tough times. Every step you make is a step toward taking control of your life. You get to decide what grief looks like in your personal space and put it in a proper place. God did not place you here to manage your problems alone. He has provided you with a circle of love that starts with Him. Reach up and receive all that He has to offer, and watch your strength increase day by day!

Pain to Purpose Exercise

List five things you have learned about your grief over the past 30 days. How will you incorporate them on your journey?

Prayer

"*Father, I want to thank You for taking me through this experience. Thank You for teaching me that I am not alone and that I am never alone. Help me to adopt what I've learned and apply it to my everyday life. Lord, thank You for future opportunities that I can share with others what you have shown me about grief. In Jesus' name, amen.*"

REFLECTION

What did you learn from this devotional that was made clear to you about grief? How will you use the tools to manage grief?

_____

_____

_____

_____

_____

_____

_____

_____

_____

_____

_____

_____

_____

_____

ABOUT THE AUTHOR

*F*rom the sudden death of her son and a public divorce, to recovering from COVID-19 and the tragic murder of her father, Dr. Terra DeFoe knows what it's like to go from surviving to thriving. Where many people saw nothing but strongholds and struggles, she saw hope, healing and steppingstones to success. Recognized for her community service from former President Barack Obama, Dr. DeFoe has been fortunate to serve in public service and advocacy for more than 20 years—allowing her to effect change in faith-based, corporate and community organizations across the nation. Whereas many people have to "pull themselves up by their bootstraps," Dr. DeFoe was required to tan and cut the hide, stitch the soles, and weave her own bootlaces, to say the least.

Raised by her grandparents after the sudden death of her mother at the age of seventeen, life for Dr. DeFoe—in a nutshell—ain't been no crystal staircase. By the time she graduated from high school, she was the mother of two children. By the time she was twenty, she was diagnosed with dyslexia, which resulted from a work-related, closed-head injury. Full of resilience and faith, even in the midst of insurmountable grief, she made a conscious choice to bring purpose to the pain. In addition to helping others who have been swallowed by loss and death, Dr. DeFoe works diligently to help others cope with trauma by grabbing hold of a better tomorrow, one day at a time.

A certified professional coach, peer support specialist and licensed minister, Dr. DeFoe has been honored to author several books, including *Saving the Best Dance for Last, You Never Walk Alone* and her most recent work, *Easing the Pain: Overcoming the Loss of a Child.* She also hosts an informational cable television talk show called "On the Floor with Dr. Terra DeFoe" that airs on The Impact Network nationally. Having served as the Director of African American and Faith-Based Engagement for the State of Michigan during the Hillary Clinton Presidential campaign, Dr. DeFoe currently serves as a senior adviser to Mayor Mike Duggan of Detroit and CEO and founder of "Vessels of Hope." Through Vessels of Hope, she offers a unique approach to emotional healing through evidence-based, mental health practices and holistic wellness. A beacon of hope and healing for many, she is best known for helping others unlock and express unresolved toxic mental patterns and negative behavior cycles in order to create innovative solutions on a path of healing. A routine guest lecturer for the University of Michigan—Ann Arbor School of Social Work, Dr. DeFoe has a heart of gold that is unmatched when it comes to service and community advocacy.

For more information or bookings, call 313.801.6600 or email Terra@decolellc.com. You can also visit her on the web at www.iamterradefoe.com.

REFERENCES

The Bible: New International Version. (1984). International Bible Society.

Crna, R. N. M. (2022b, July 25). *Understanding the physical symptoms of grief.* Healthline. https://www.healthline.com/health/grief-physical-symptoms#moods

Bald Eagle - Denver Zoo. (2018, December 18). Denver Zoo. https://denverzoo.org/animals/bald-eagle/#:~:text=High%20Flyers,wind%20currents%20and%20thermal%20updrafts.